THE WILD SWANS

ILLUSTRATED BY
HELEN STRATTON

RETOLD BY JAMES RIORDAN

SERIES EDITOR · ELIZABETH RUDD

HUTCHINSON

LONDON · MELBOURNE · AUCKLAND · JOHANNESBURG

This edition published in Great Britain in 1987
by Hutchinson Children's Books
An imprint of Century Hutchinson Ltd
Brookmount House, 62-65 Chandos Place,
Covent Garden, London WC2N 4NW

Century Hutchinson Australia (Pty) Ltd
16-22 Church Street, Hawthorn, Melbourne,
Victoria 3122

Century Hutchinson New Zealand Limited
32-34 View Road, PO Box 40-086, Glenfield,
Auckland 10

Century Hutchinson South Africa (Pty) Ltd
PO Box 337, Bergvlei 2012, South Africa

Designed by ACE Limited

Set in Goudy Old Style by
Rowland Phototypesetting (London) Ltd

Printed and bound in Italy

ISBN 0 09 172549 6

In a land far away, where swallows go in wintertime, there lived a king and queen who had one daughter and eleven sons. The sons would go to school with stars on their chests and swords at their sides; they would write on blocks of gold with diamond pens and know their lessons off by heart. You could tell at once that they were princes.

Their sister Elise, meanwhile, would sit at home upon a little stool made of crystal glass, reading a precious picture book that cost half a kingdom. How contented the children were. But there was no way that it could last.

One day their mother died and the king remarried, this time to an evil queen who was cruel to the poor children. It began the first day she entered the palace. Instead of baked apples and cakes she gave them cupfuls of sand. 'Make believe that it's something nice,' she said spitefully.

Within a week she had sent little Elise away to live with peasants in the forest. And she so filled the king's head with wicked tales about his sons that he soon turned against them.

'Away with you,' cried the evil queen. 'Fly about the world as great dumb birds.'

But her powers were not great enough to do them all the harm that she wished, and instead they turned into beautiful wild swans. With an unfamiliar cry, they flew from the palace window, over the gardens and away into the forest.

It was early morning when they reached the cottage where Elise lay asleep in her little bed. They circled low above the roof, craning their long necks to catch a glimpse of their sister and flapping their great wings to wake her up.

But she did not see or hear them. And so they had to fly on, up into the clouds, far away beyond the dense, dark forest that stretched down to the sea.

Little Elise spent her days playing on the bare floorboards of the cottage. One day passed just like another. The wind would stir the roses, murmuring, 'Who could be prettier than you?'

'Why, Elise,' came the roses' reply.

And when the wind rustled the pages of the peasant woman's book, as she sat there in the doorway watching Elise playing, it would whisper, 'Who could be as good as you?'

Back came the answer, 'Why, Elise.'

It was the truth.

When Elise turned fifteen she was taken back to the palace, and when the queen saw how beautiful she had become she was full of spite and hate. Gladly she would have turned her into a wild swan too, but she dared not do so straight away, for the king would want to see his daughter.

So next morning early, before Elise was awake, the queen took three frogs with her to the bathroom, with its marble floor and benches covered in costly cushions. She kissed one frog, saying, 'When Elise is in the bath, sit upon her head and she'll become as lazy as you.'

Kissing the second frog, she said, 'Sit upon her forehead and she'll become so ugly her father won't recognize her.'

Then she kissed the third frog. 'Sit upon her breast so that evil fills her soul.'

Then she dropped the slimy frogs into the clear bath water, which at once turned green. That done, she woke Elise and led her to the bath. 'Have a good wash, my dear,' she said. 'You must be clean for your father.'

As the girl lay back in the bath, the three frogs did the queen's bidding. One hopped on to Elise's head. One settled on her brow. One sat upon her breast. But Elise did not even notice them. And as she rose from the bath there, floating on the water instead of frogs, were three red poppies.

So cross was the evil queen that she quickly rubbed the girl with walnut juice until her body was dark brown; then she smeared her face and head with stinking grease. Surely no one would recognize her now?

When her father set eyes on her he grew alarmed and swore Elise was not his daughter. No one in the palace knew her save the loyal watchdog and the swallows. But what could such dumb creatures do to save her?

Poor Elise wept. She wondered where her eleven brothers could be; what had the wicked queen done to them? In despair she stole out of the palace and walked all through the day, over meadows and swamps, until she came to the dense, dark forest. She had no idea which way to go. She only knew she was sad and lonely and longed to see her brothers once again. She made up her mind to find them.

Night descended as she entered the forest and she sank down upon soft moss to sleep, using a tree stump for a pillow. All through the night she dreamed of her brothers: of them as children writing with their diamond pens upon the blocks of gold, of herself reading her picture book. But in her dream it was not sums her brothers were doing, they were describing their adventures, all they had seen and done. Her picture book came to life: birds sang, people stepped from the pages to talk to her.

When she awoke, the sun was already high in the sky. The green wood smelt so fresh and the birds were so friendly that her spirits rose at once.

Hearing water splashing nearby, she followed the narrow streams that led to a pool, so clear she could see the sandy bottom. As she gazed into the water she saw trees and bushes: if they had not swayed gently in the breeze she might have thought they were painted on the water, so perfect was the reflection.

But the moment she saw her own face she recoiled in alarm at the dirty, ugly sight. She threw off her clothes at once and bathed in the cool water until there was none lovelier in the whole wide world than the fair princess.

When she had dressed and plaited her long, smooth hair, she walked on through the forest, the thought of her brothers gave her strength and hope. She had not gone far when she met an old woman with a wooden staff and a basketful of red berries. The woman offered her some.

'Thank you,' Elise said. 'I wonder, have you seen eleven princes riding through the forest?'

'No,' the woman replied, 'but I did see eleven swans with gold crowns swimming in a river close by. I'll show you the spot.'

She led Elise through the trees and up a steep bank that overhung a winding stream. Elise bade farewell to the woman, descended the steep slope and followed the stream until its waters met the sea.

Spread before her was the boundless ocean; yet she could see no sails, no boats on the shore. How could she journey on? She gazed at the countless pebbles on the beach, rounded and polished by the sea.

'It keeps on rolling, tirelessly, grinding and polishing even the hardest stone,' she said to herself. 'The sea has given me strength. Thank you, Waves, for the lesson you have taught me. Some day I know you will carry me to my dear brothers.'

Amongst the tangled seaweed on the shore she found eleven swan feathers which she gathered in her hand. To each clung a drop of water – whether tears or dew she could not tell.

Then as the sun sank down slowly beyond the sea, Elise saw eleven swans, gold crowns upon their heads, flying towards her. Like white kites being pulled across the sky, they came gliding one behind the other. Afraid of startling them, she hid behind a bush, watching them land nearby, beating their great white wings.

The moment the sun sank out of sight, the swans all at once turned into handsome princes. They were Elise's brothers. She let out a cry of joy, for although they were now grown up she recognized them at once, and rushed to greet them. They cried with joy at seeing their sister, now grown into a beautiful young woman.

By day we have to fly as swans,' the eldest brother said. 'Only at nightfall do we regain our human form. That is why we must never be in flight at sunset, for we would fall and be killed when we turn to men.

'The land in which we live lies beyond the clutches of the evil queen: it is across the ocean, far, far away. Since there is no island in between we cannot rest during our long journey. However, midway across the sea a lone rock juts above the waves; it is just big enough to hold us all, huddled together. If it were not for the rock we would never be able to visit our beloved home. As it is, our journey takes two whole days and we can fly here once a year in midsummer when the days are long.

'We may remain eleven days, just enough time to fly across the dense, dark forest to see our father's palace and visit our mother's grave. That is why we return to the land of our birth. And now we have found you, dear sister.'

They talked on through the night, snatching only a brief sleep. Elise awoke to the sound of wings beating the air: her brothers had turned back to swans and were circling above her before flying off beyond the trees. Only the youngest brother remained, resting his head in her lap as she stroked his strong, white wings. Towards evening the others returned, taking their human form as the red sun slowly set.

'Tomorrow we must fly away,' the eldest brother said. 'We dare not stay longer. But we cannot leave you behind, dear Elise.'

'Oh, do take me with you,' Elise cried.

They spent the entire night weaving a bed of birch bark supported by a net of rugged reeds. When it was ready Elise lay down upon it and was so tired she fell asleep at once. As the sun came up the princes turned back to swans, picked up the net in their beaks and rose into the sky with their sleeping sister. And so that the sun did not burn her face, one swan flew above her to shade her with his wings.

They were far out to sea when Elise awoke. At first she thought she was dreaming, it felt so strange to sail through the air, high in the sky. Being hungry, she noticed beside her a branch of full, ripe berries and some sweet roots. It was her youngest brother who had gathered them; and it was he who now flew above her to protect her from the sun.

All day long the wild swans sped like arrows through the air. But they were now tiring fast and, to add to their plight, dark clouds on the horizon warned of a coming storm. Anxiously, Elise watched the sun sinking; she searched the sea in vain for the lonely rock.

Now the swans' wings were beating more slowly and they were losing height. It would be her fault if the sun set and they all fell to their deaths, drowning in the sea.

Still no rock could be seen. Black storm clouds filled the sky. Elise could feel the heavy breath of the approaching storm; the waves had turned the colour of lead, lightning flashed and thunder boomed. Poor Elise shivered with fear.

Half the sun had sunk beneath the waves and Elise spotted the little rock. They landed safely just as the sun gave one last defiant flare, before going out. Her brothers linked hands around her.

There was scarcely room for them all. Waves beat against the rock and burst over them like a shower of rain; lightning lit up the sky and thunder claps deafened them. But they held hands firmly and bravely sang to keep their spirits high.

At dawn the storm was over, leaving the air fresh and clear. As soon as the sun rose the swans took off with Elise on her birch-bark bed. The sea was still rough, so that as she gazed below she saw white foam upon a dark-green sea.

As the sun climbed higher, Elise was surprised to see a strange sight before her floating in the sky: a mountainous land of snow and glittering ice, with an enormous castle of pillars. Below it were wooded slopes of waving palms and flowers. 'Is this the fair land where you live?' she asked her brothers.

They shook their heads. 'No,' explained her eldest brother. 'It is only a mirage, a castle in the air, ever changing shape. No mortal can ever go there.'

At last Elise spied land in the distance: the hills of cedar forests shone blue in the clear light of afternoon. They flew over castles and towns until, finally, in the early evening shadows, she found herself sitting on a hillside before a cave overgrown with vines and plants like some gigantic tapestry.

'You must be tired,' said her youngest brother, taking her to a bed inside the cave. 'Sleep now and then tomorrow you can tell us what you dreamed.'

'If only I could dream of how to set you free,' she said.

As she slept she imagined she was flying to the castle in the air where a fairy welcomed her. She resembled the old woman Elise had met in the wood, the one who had told her of the wild swans.

'You may free your brothers,' said the fairy, 'if you are brave and strong enough. Do you see this stinging nettle in my hand? There are many about the cave where you are sleeping, and in the graveyard too; you must pick them even though they sting and blister your hands. Then you must tread the nettles with your feet to turn them into flax from which you must make yarn. With that yarn you must knit eleven shirts; the moment you throw a shirt over each wild swan you'll break the spell.

'But heed one thing more: from the moment you begin your task until it is finished, you must stay silent – no matter how long it takes you. Should you utter a single word, it will pierce your brothers' hearts like a dagger.'

So saying, the fairy touched Elise's hand with the stinging nettle, waking her up at once. It was midday. Near the mouth of the cave grew a bed of nettles, just like those she had seen in her sleep. At once she set to picking them with her bare hands. All the same, she would gladly bear the pain if only she could free her brothers.

When her brothers arrived at sunset they were alarmed to find her dumb and silent. But when they saw her arms and legs all covered in red blisters, they realized she was engaged on some important task. The youngest brother wept, and as his tears fell upon her hands and feet, the pain and blisters disappeared.

All night long she worked without cease, and through the next day, too. By twilight the first of the nettle shirts was done.

Next day she caught the sound of hunting horns up in the hills above the cave. It grew louder, and suddenly before her was a group of huntsmen, led by a handsome king. 'What are you doing here?' he demanded.

Elise shook her head dumbly. She could not speak for fear of risking her brothers' lives.

'We cannot leave you here,' said the king. 'Come with us, and if you are as good as you are fair you shall be clad in silk and velvet, wear a golden crown upon your head and live in the finest palace.'

Then he lifted her on to his horse.

By evening they had reached the royal city with its fine mansions and handsome churches. Elise did not see them through the bitter tears that blurred her eyes. Silently she let maids dress her in royal gowns, plait her hair with pearls and draw long gloves upon her blistered hands.

When at last she stood before the king the whole court bowed and curtsied low before her dazzling beauty, and the king announced her as his queen. Only the archbishop shook his head, muttering that this wild forest maid must be a witch who had cast a spell upon the king.

Ignoring him, the king commanded the musicians to play and the feasting to commence. Yet not a smile graced Elise's lips, not a spark of wonder shone in her eyes. Her face was full of anguish and despair. Only when the king took her to a little chamber did Elise look at him with gratitude. The little room was just like the cave she had shared with her brothers; in one corner lay the green yarn she had spun from nettles, and from a rafter hung the shirt already done.

'You may dream in here that you are back home,' said the king. As Elise gazed upon her beloved handiwork, the colour came back into her cheeks. Thinking of her poor brothers, she kissed the king's hand in gratitude.

That so pleased the king he ordered all the church bells to be rung and the wedding to be proclaimed throughout the land without any more ado.

Gradually, Elise's eyes began to shine with love for the handsome king who did all he could to please her. Each day her love grew stronger. If only she could tell him of her sorrow. But she had to complete her task in silence; that she knew well.

At night, while the king slept, she would go to the little room in the palace tower to weave the nettle shirts for her brothers. Yet as she began the seventh shirt, she ran out of yarn.

With fear in her heart, she crept out of the palace in the dead of night, made her way through deserted streets and into the church graveyard. It was a bright, moonlit night and as she passed a large tombstone she stopped in her tracks: for there upon a grave sat a group of hideous witches.

Elise had to walk past them, but though they fixed their eyes upon her, they did her no harm. She quickly gathered a bundle of nettles and returned to the palace.

But someone had seen her: it was the archbishop, he who watched while others slept. He was now certain his suspicions had been correct: the queen was a witch.

When next the king went to church, the archbishop told him of his fears and what he had seen. He spoke so spitefully that the carved images of the saints all shook their heads, as if to say, 'No, no, Elise is innocent.'

The king, however, thought they shook their heads in sorrow at her sin. Two tears rolled down his cheeks as he returned to the palace. That night he pretended to be asleep and, as Elise rose, he followed her. Every night she did the same and each time he followed her unobserved, watching her disappear into the little room.

As each day passed the king's heart grew heavier. Elise noticed his sadness, though she did not guess its cause; thoughts of her brothers filled her mind. But her task would soon be done, for only one shirt had to be made. Alas, her yarn again was finished. She would have to go to the churchyard one last time.

As Elise made her way to the graveyard, the king and archbishop followed close behind. They watched as she passed through the churchyard gates and approached the hags squatting on a grave. The king turned away, sick at heart, certain now that Elise was a witch. 'Let the people pass judgement!' he proclaimed.

The people judged her guilty. 'Burn her at the stake!' they cried.

Elise was cast into a dungeon where the wind whistled through the iron bars. Instead of silk and velvet, they gave her nettles as a pillow and the spun shirts as a blanket. Straight away she set to work on the final shirt, while street urchins mocked and called her names. No one had a word of comfort for her.

As the sun was sinking she caught the swish of swans' wings beating upon the bars. It was her youngest brother; he had found her at last. She wept for joy. Although this was to be her last night alive, her work was almost done and her brothers would receive their shirts.

Just at that moment the archbishop entered the dungeon to spend a last few hours with the prisoner. But she shook her head firmly and pointed to the door. She had to complete her work that night or all the pain and torment would be in vain.

She set to work on the shirt. Little mice scurried to and fro, fetching nettles, eager to help. A thrush sang by the iron bars all through the night, to keep her spirits up.

One hour before daybreak, her brothers went to the palace to see the king. But the guards barred the way. Could it not wait till morning? But the princes made such a noise that they woke up the king, who came himself to investigate. Just as he stepped outside the gate, the sun rose and the visitors disappeared. And the king saw only eleven wild swans, flying above the palace roof.

Soon the city was awake and filled with people bustling through the streets to see the witch burnt at the stake. An old nag drew the cart in which Elise sat. Elise was dressed in sackcloth, her long chestnut hair hanging loose about her lovely form, and her face deathly pale. Her lips moved in silent prayer for her brothers, as her fingers wove the last green shirt; the other ten lay at her feet.

But the people who lined the way jeered and mocked her, 'Look at the witch mumbling her spells. Her hands hold witchcraft, not a Bible. Tear it from her! Tear it to pieces!'

The mob tried to stop the cart and snatch Elise's work, and they would have succeeded had swans not swooped down and landed on the cart, beating the air with their strong wings. The people drew back in fear.

'It's a sign she is innocent,' some murmured low, though they dared not speak aloud.

As the executioner went to lead her to the stake, she broke free and hastily cast the shirts over the eleven swans.

And there, as the crowd gasped, stood eleven proud princes with gold crowns. The youngest, however, had a swan's wing for an arm, for Elise had not had time to finish his shirt.

Then she stood up and cried out for all to hear, 'Now I can speak. Hear me: I am innocent.'

The people who witnessed this miracle knelt down before her. Elise, overcome with fear and pain, collapsed into her brothers' arms.

'She is indeed innocent,' cried the eldest brother. And he recounted all that had happened.

As he was speaking, a heady perfume of roses filled the air: for every piece of wood about the stake had taken root and blossomed, surrounding Elise with dark red roses. At the very top of the bush bloomed a single rose, white and gleaming like the morning star.

Stepping forward, the king plucked it and placed it on Elise's breast; and she turned towards him, smiling, with peace and joy filling her heart.

All at once church bells rang out of their own accord and flocks of birds filled the sky. No one had ever seen such a grand procession as the one that moved through the streets: Elise and the king at the head, followed by the proud princes, one with a swan's wing for an arm, then the archbishop, his head bowed low in shame and, finally, the royal courtiers.

How the good folk cheered. Of course, they had known Elise to be innocent all along.

Our story does not end here. For not long after, the eleven princes set out in a ship for their own land. And in no time at all they freed their realm of the wicked queen: she drowned in the marble bath with her frogs.

And all are living happily to this day in the land beyond the sea.